My grandma and

by Jenny Giles
Photography by Bill Thomas

I am going to stay
with Grandma and Grandpa.

My mom and dad
are going away for two days.

I like staying with Grandma
and Grandpa.

My pajamas
and my toothbrush
are in my bag.
My teddy bear
is in my bag, too.

Grandma is good at cooking.

I like helping her.

Grandma makes little cakes
for all of us.

We like eating Grandma's cakes.

Grandpa plays soccer
with me.
He is good at soccer.

I can run and kick the ball
to Grandpa.

We make houses with cards.

We make big houses
and little houses.

This is where I sleep
at Grandma and Grandpa's house.

My toys are in a box.

Can you see the photo of me?

My grandma and grandpa love me.
They like looking after me.